MW00957936

Master Critical Thinking for Teens

The Complete Guide to Improving Decision-Making
Skills, Mastering Problem Solving, and Conquering
Logical Fallacies

Jake Johnson

Table of Contents

Introduction   1

Chapter 1: Critical Thinking: An Introduction   5

Benefits of Critical Thinking 6

How to Utilize Critical Thinking in the Decision-Making Process.. 13

Chapter 2: Bias and Logical Fallacies   20

What Is Bias? 22

Types of Biases 22

Logical Fallacies 29

How to Recognize and Avoid Biases and Logical Fallacies 38

Chapter 3: Inspecting Your Sources   41

Evaluating Our Sources 42

Locating Reliable Resources 47

Chapter 4: Asking the Right Questions   56

Why Questions Are Important 57

Asking Effective Questions That Get to The Bottom of Things 58

Practice 62

Chapter 5: Analyzing Arguments   65

Steps For Analyzing An Argument 66

Determining an Argument's Validity 71

Chapter 6: Applying Critical Thinking to Real World Situations   74

Social Media and Online Websites 75

Media Messages and Advertisements 78

Making Informed Decisions 81

Chapter 7: Tips For Improving Critical Thinking Skills   85

Read Everything You Can Get Your Hands On 85

Expose Yourself to Diverse Perspectives 87

Practice Questioning and Analyzing Arguments 88

Identify Your Own Biases 89

Listen For Logical Fallacies 90

Practice Active Listening 91

Chapter 8: Exercises   93

Exercise 1: Analyzing a Political Advertisement 93

Exercise 2: Analyzing a Health Claim 97

Exercise 3: Evaluating an Argumentative Essay 100

Conclusion   103

References   106

Introduction

It's safe to say that teenage years aren't easy. There's a lot going on, and the expectations seem to increase while personal freedom does not. Your understanding of the world and your role in it are drastically increasing and yet, no one seems to notice. Why?

For me, it was about expressing this increase. I had more knowledge and understanding than others realized, but what I didn't know was how to speak "adult," and show them that I knew these things.

Parents and teachers may not be willing to consider what you have to say on the matter. They've already had a lot of life experience that has shown them what to believe. Your different experience may tell you something else, but with long formed opinions, they find it hard to consider your opinion. For instance, I remember arguing with my teachers many times over the use of specific sources, such as Wikipedia, for papers. While much of the information can be fact-checked, I found it's often treated by teachers as an unreliable source because anyone can contribute to it.

Not only do we often have our teachers and parents to contend with, but there are also people like our siblings, friends, and even the people we briefly meet each day. If you have siblings, you know that it's almost impossible to agree with each other. It feels like they often disagree just because they want to disagree with us. Our friends might be new or people we've been friends with since childhood. No matter how long a friendship might have gone on, there is a chance that a single issue could end it.

Most of the people we meet in person want the best for us. They are there to support us in achieving our goals while we, in turn, support them. The same cannot be said for the people we know, but don't meet.

You've probably heard the phrase "don't believe everything you see on the internet," but most of us just apply that to the things we see that clearly aren't true. For example, if you read something about a mysterious figure lurking in a park, you are likely to question it because this is, after all, the internet.

But, what about social media? Do we question the pictures of our favorite influencers? Do we question why they always seem so happy and well put together? The answer is often no, and we tend go so far as to compare ourselves to creators. The harm is often to our mental health, especially our self-esteem (Laplante, 2022). For example, you open Instagram, and you see one of your favorite influencers making an acai bowl with all the extras. It looks artsy and fun and all you can do is stare at your own bowl of cereal. What you might not know is that they did this, and many of their other photos in a single workday. It wasn't a spur of the moment breakfast at all!

This also holds true for advertisements. Today, advertisements are everywhere, including billboards, commercials, 30 second ads on platforms like TikTok and YouTube, other social platforms, and more. While most ads contain a different advertised product, nearly every ad is doing the same thing, and that is claiming that it will fix something in your life. In most cases, the product doesn't work as well as advertised but, in some instances, it has ended up being harmful to the buyer.

A cross between influencers and advertisers is politicians. As you approach the age to vote, you might have had a few questions about the political sphere and how your vote matters. However, when you watch anything related to it, or try to make sense of what everyone is saying, all you often find is one side calling the other a liar (and maybe, occasionally, they will promise to fix something).

I can speak from experience when I say that as you leave your teen years, there are still a lot of things that won't fit into place right away, and to get past that, critical thinking skills are an absolute must.

Critical thinking can help you gather and explain your viewpoint to the authority figures around you in a way that will make them listen. It can help you when you're stuck in place with a friendship. It can help you sort through social media, ads, news stories, and often even politics.

One of the best things about it is that it helps you gain knowledge, new insights, and even find solutions that you might not have even considered otherwise.

Critical thinking can be great if you know how to use it!

CHAPTER 1

Critical Thinking: An Introduction

When I was younger, I lived near the woods. There were plenty of creatures around since it was their natural habitat, but a common pest was snakes. They liked to hide in the small crevices around the house. I remember being told that snakes were harmless. They couldn't hurt me, so there was no need to bug them. If they were smaller, we could pick them up if we were gentle. Now, as an adult, I have access to more information. I am by no means scared of snakes, but I know that I probably shouldn't pick one up unless I want to get bitten. Critical thinking does play a role in this. With it, I know that even though I've had certain life experiences, the experience of others outweighs that.

Critical thinking has a lot of definitions. The best one I have found says that critical thinking is a dedication to finding and understanding the truth of any situation (Foundation for Critical Thinking, n.d.). This means that no matter what we are working with, even if the subject is small, we consider all the elements. If we don't, we might miss something crucial to the truth.

My own example is snakes. I have plenty of life experience to tell me that handling one is fine, but even a small amount of research can tell me the truth about them. While the ones near my house were small and possibly used to being randomly picked up by small children, many would be very angry if they were randomly removed from their habitat, and they would probably attack. Critical thinking has many applications beyond this though. In your own life, you might already be able to think of some examples, but how much further can it go?

Benefits of Critical Thinking

Helps With Communication

Critical thinking can help you break down barriers in communication. As already stated, when we're practicing critical thinking, we need to look at all the elements of the subject we are thinking about. This includes considering other points of view.

Imagine a common issue that you go back and forth on with your parents. They think one thing, and you think another. Take a deep breath, and then try to put yourself in their shoes. As you start to do so, you might feel a tinge of defensiveness creep up, especially if this is a hot issue in your home right now. If it does, just try to take a deep breath and move past it. Your goal is to try to completely understand their viewpoint without feeling that intrinsic defensiveness. This can help in a few ways: While it may not change your own viewpoint, it can help you be more sympathetic to theirs. If they can see that you do understand their view, but you still don't agree, then they may be more willing to return that favor.

Now, if you can understand their viewpoint, and remain calm as you think it over, then you can bring that feeling into a discussion over the issue. It's not uncommon for another person to try to move you to defend your own stance rather than focus on any weak points in theirs. Adults especially can be good at doing this. If you keep your exterior calm, it will be a lot harder for anyone to do this.

Finally, if you have a full understanding of the other person's point of view, you can better refute it with your own. For example, your parents might not be okay with you going to an event late at night. You are attending with several friends, many of whom you've been friends with for years, and you don't see the issue. They have concerns about your safety and security, and they are worried that you might try to do something they wouldn't approve of. By fully understanding their view, you can refute it by letting them know that you will be there with several friends, many of which they know and trust, and you can point out that you haven't done anything to break their trust so far, so why would you start now?

These points apply not only to your communication with older adults, but also with your friends and siblings.

Expanding Creativity

Critical thinking applications go beyond just thinking in a classroom or winning an argument. It will help you expand your creativity.

When it comes to being creative, there isn't really a specific truth to discover. Instead, you are going after your own truth in any way you wish. With expanded critical thinking skills, you are thinking of all possible elements that could go into your truth.

This can apply to the academic field. You might be struggling in math class and remember a different way to get the answer, thanks to critical thinking. You might be doing a science experiment and figure out the best way to get the reaction you want, or you might think of a completely new take on your book in English class.

You can get into your creative hobbies as well. Something as simple as a painting can be elevated by critical thinking because you are challenging yourself to use different tools and techniques.

There are a variety of different hobbies out there, and many of them can be influenced by critical thinking.

New Insights

In cartoons, we see this happen quite literally. The character is thinking deeply about their predicament when suddenly, a light bulb goes off over their head. They have an idea!

While a light bulb may not literally appear over our heads, critical thinking can create moments like this for us.

You're being encouraged to explore all the possibilities, even the ones that seem like they wouldn't work for any reason. If you think a little further out of the box than something might require, you may stumble upon the perfect answer to your question. Sometimes the answer simply solves a minor problem, while other times it creates new ideas entirely. For example, have you ever wondered about the creation of the internet?

If you were to participate in some outside-of-the-box thinking, what do you think you would come up with?

Better Problem-Solving Skills

As we grow up, we run into more and more problems. Some are fun to solve, like what you might choose for a career, while others can be less fun. Critical thinking can help you become a better problem solver because it takes you through all those extra steps so that you know you are making a good decision. A person who doesn't regularly practice critical thinking might neglect certain sections because they don't feel they are important or they forget to consider them altogether, but the roadmap for problem solving can help you avoid these traps. We will talk about this in the next section!

Curiosity

The more we think critically and find things like expanded creativity or new insights, the more we start to enjoy it. Critical thinking becomes natural, even if certain problems don't directly involve you. You might even pick up new knowledge from the most mundane of places. It all comes together to make you more curious and, as a result, you will discover new things!

You Become More Self-Reliant

One thing critical thinking will teach you is to assume everyone is wrong until proven right. This includes social media, ads, websites, friends, and sometimes even parents or teachers. If you are told something and you're expected to take it as a fact, try to check it first. See if you can find something that confirms what you're hearing. We will go more into detail about how this applies to the world of academics further down the road, but a major benefit of this is that you know the facts you have are correct, and you're not depending on others to give you some potentially false information.

Confidence

This is more of a side effect of critical thinking, and it sure is a great one. When you expand your creativity, you are showing yourself that you can produce great things. When you can communicate with others in a better way, you are able to be heard. When you are consciously checking facts before accepting them, you're increasing your independence. All of this creates more self-confidence.

Self-Reflection

As humans, we must admit that we aren't perfect all the time. Sometimes the consequences are small or insignificant, but other times our actions hurt others. At the moment, our actions may have made sense, but when we look back, we realize that there might have been some unintended damage.

Without critical thinking, we might try to ignore this or brush it off. With critical thinking, we do question even our own actions.

By committing to doing this, we ensure, first off, that our actions don't seriously harm others, and if they have, we recognize it and apologize. We may also become more aware of the consequence our actions have on ourselves.

Another beauty of self-reflection is that when we see how one course of action takes effect, we can plan on what we might do differently this time. That doesn't just apply to potentially upsetting others. It also means that we can reflect on plans that didn't quite turn out so well, failed school projects, and more.

Think about it. If you fail a test, you might be upset. With critical thinking, you will be motivated to think about what you might do differently to get a better result rather than beating yourself up about what has already come to pass.

Increasing Respect

Respect goes a long way toward gaining trust and freedom. As a teen, this is tough. A lot of people deal out respect based on life experience, which is hard to come by when we are younger. Because of this, we need to find other ways to gain that.

Critical thinking can be a great way. When you utilize critical thinking, you are constantly making decisions based on evidence that you have. You're considering all viewpoints, including the ones you don't agree with. A lot of your views and opinions are based on critical thought, and if someone asks you about them, you have an answer ready. It pulls you through debates, disagreements, and it often shows when you do your schoolwork.

When these skills become necessary, you can show that you have them. The more often it happens, the more respect you will gain. While this process sounds like it might take a long time, it might not. Make sure you are ready for what is next, and you can seek out opportunities to show what you know if you need to.

Critical thinking has some far-reaching applications, but one of the biggest is decision making.

How to Utilize Critical Thinking in the Decision-Making Process

Critical thinking plays a key role when it comes to decision making. By utilizing it, you can assure that you are making the best decisions you can with the information that you have, and you can learn from your experience.

To start, we're going to join Lupe for a decision. Lupe is choosing her classes for the upcoming school year and this year she needs to pick a language. Her school offers French, Spanish, American Sign Language (ASL), and German. Lupe herself is a native English speaker, but her family background is much more interesting. Her grandparents were immigrants from Mexico, and they speak fluent Spanish. So do her parents. Additionally, her five-year-old brother is deaf. The entire family has been working to learn ASL, and Lupe thinks that the additional class might help. A final thing for Lupe to take into consideration is that she desperately wants to visit France someday. She's studied the culture and some of the artists, and her room is decorated with art that depicts different attractions in France.

Now that you know the situation, let's look at how critical thinking can help us, and Lupe, make a decision or solve the dilemma she is facing.

Step 1

The first step is the critical thinking process to understand what the problem is, or what decision we are trying to make. We need to consider all the facts at hand that affect this decision too.

The facts in this case are that Lupe is a third-generation immigrant and learning Spanish could lead to great communication with her relatives. Her brother is deaf, so learning ASL could be beneficial as well. Finally, going to France is a dream of hers and it would help to know the language. All of these affect the decision that Lupe would make.

Step 2

Once we have all the facts laid out, we can determine what our options are. It's important to lay out every single possibility, even if it doesn't seem like it's going to happen. If we cross something out too early, we might miss a great opportunity.

In Lupe's case, she has four choices. She can study Spanish, ASL, French, or German. If you were in a position like Lupe's, you'd likely keep German in the cards, even if it doesn't feel like the option you'd chose.

Now, we need to examine what biases we have, where they come from, and what factors have influenced them. It's normal to have biases that affect our ability to make decisions. As a part of critical thinking, we must acknowledge what these biases are.

In Lupe's case, the bias is her desire to learn French. She wants to learn it so that she can have an easier time visiting the country.

Some biases will make a difference in your decision and in Lupe's case, they should. Other biases, however, might negatively affect your choice if they were included in the decision-making process.

Step 3

Once we decide what our options are, it's time to consider what about each decision makes it a good one, and what the drawbacks are.

Let's illustrate this in Lupe's decision.

First off is German. It's an offered class but it doesn't seem to have any other draws to it. The drawback to choosing German over other subjects is that she loses out on the chance to communicate more with her extended family, her brother, and she loses the chance to learn a language that might help her later.

If she studies Spanish, she does learn some of her family's native language, which would allow her better communication with her extended relatives. Additionally, if she needed help with homework, there would be several people on standby that would be more than willing. The drawbacks are that she loses out on the opportunity to gain ground in communicating with her brother, and she loses the chance to learn a language for later.

ASL is almost the same. She can learn for her brother, while losing out on the other two options.

Finally, in the case of learning French, Lupe knows that she will enjoy the class, and when she is able to visit France later in life, she will have an easier time getting around. But she loses the chance to communicate with her family and her brother.

Step 4

Now that you have all your information together, you can weigh each decision and its draw and drawbacks and choose whatever is going to be in your best interest.

Lupe would weigh each decision, and while she would likely eliminate German quickly, the others may take her some time.

Step 5

This step could come a bit later, depending on what your decision was. Once you have decided, let it play out. Then, come back to it. What did you learn from this decision? Was there anything you could have done differently? Given the option, would you make the same decision again?

This final step helps us learn from our decisions so that we can make better decisions in our future.

Now, this can feel like a lot of steps. To be honest, it is. But, by following this process, you make yourself stop and think rather than acting rashly on a decision. You may end up making a better choice for yourself, and if you follow through, you will learn something from your decision.

As much work as it seems, I have found that it's always been worth it.

I have found that by using critical thinking, I was able to form a more understanding relationship with my parents and teachers. This sometimes meant that I was able to talk my way into getting a higher grade or being able to go to an event when my parents initially said no. If I couldn't come to an agreement with the authority figures in my life, I was at least able to understand their side and they were able to understand mine. I learned how to build better relationships based on thoughtfulness and trust with my friends and siblings too. These in-person relationships became something to rely on as we entered a new online era.

Toward the end of my teen years, I was especially vulnerable to online media. It's very easy to believe everything we see, even though what's on social media is rarely the truth. Critical thinking won't tell you what to believe, but it can give you the right facts and you can form your own opinions from there. Not only does this matter when we're talking about social media, but it becomes extremely important later when you're able to vote.

A common issue in politics is the use of logical fallacies. You can find these anywhere. It doesn't matter what side of the political spectrum you're studying. Logical fallacies aren't just prevalent in politics either. Parents, friends, teachers, future employers, and anyone else you might meet down the line can all be guilty of using logical fallacies to try to get their way. Whether you're getting ready to vote soon or if you're just trying to navigate hidden cues in conversations, knowing about logical fallacies can go a long way.

CHAPTER 2

Bias and Logical Fallacies

Logical fallacies and biases can be tough to spot. They are committed every day, often right in front of us. To avoid falling victim to one, you need to know what you face.

It's also important to remember that you might be making use of these, without even realizing it.

Emily had been stuck in an argument with her teacher for over a week. She'd been struggling in school because of her parents' divorce, and it was showing in her grades. Realizing that she needed to get them up so she could move up to the next grade, Emily hired a tutor. Her tutor helped her with one assignment, but when she turned it in, her teacher noticed the sudden increase in quality, and he accused Emily of cheating. He didn't have any other evidence, but he was firm in his belief. Given her situation, he pulled Emily aside and informed her of his accusation. He offered not to tell the principal so that it wouldn't reflect badly on her, but she would still get a zero. Given the size of the assignment, it meant that Emily's chance of failing the class increased significantly.

When she pointed out that he didn't have any evidence, he told her that her increase was too big. He also mentioned that a student from a divorced household had cheated the previous semester, and that it was a common issue among students with separating families. Emily couldn't believe it. She tried going to another teacher for help, but they admitted that they were taking that teacher's side in the matter. This upset Emily, and she mentioned it to a friend's parent who suggested that she take it to the principal.

Emily was initially worried that the principal would take the teacher's side as well. She made sure to mention that this was an additional stress on top of her family struggles, and that the school board wouldn't like that she was being given a zero when there wasn't any proof that Emily cheated on the assignment.

In this encounter, there are several examples of bias and a couple of logical fallacies as well. Some were committed by the teachers, and some by Emily herself.

To make sound arguments as well as to better refute others, it's best that we avoid these.

What Is Bias?

Bias is something that you subconsciously hold onto even if there is little to no evidence to support this bias. For example, the belief that the elderly are bad at technology is a common bias. It's a stereotype, which bias is often bound up in. It may seem like a harmless one to hold, especially if you are often helping your grandparents with questions on their devices, but this bias has led to some people who are great at technology getting denied jobs just because they are older.

Biases like these can hurt critical thinking.

Types of Biases

Look at this list and think for a moment. Some of these might be recognizable.

Social Bias

Social bias is a train of thought that pertains to a group in a way that alienates someone, whether it be that other person, or the one committing the social bias. The example with the elderly is a social bias.

Now, there are some ugly examples of social bias. These include racism, sexism, religious hatred and oppression, homophobia, and sadly many others. These are often easier to spot, but there are some ways that social bias can creep in without us noticing.

Let's revisit Emily's story. While she's trying to deal with the issue, she goes to another teacher and mentions the struggle that she's having. Even though there isn't any evidence, the other teacher sides with her accuser. This is what's called ingroup bias. We are more likely to believe someone within our group than we are to believe an outsider.

The teacher that Emily tried to talk to didn't believe her, and it was largely due to the fact that she was inclined to believe her fellow teacher rather than a student.

When we let ourselves get caught up in social bias, we miss a lot of information. We're more likely to get things wrong due to blind trust. As you might have already witnessed, social bias has created some widespread issues. These can go all the way to influencing certain laws. For example, many people believe that people are poor because they are lazy. What we might not think about is a lack of education, injuries and disability, or that children could be creating the financial strain. Yet, this belief has made its way into policy, making any sort of assistance hard to get.

As you go through the critical thought process, always think of any social biases that you might be holding onto, and how they might be affecting your judgment.

Emotional Bias

Emotional bias is easy to spot if you are not the one engaging in it.

Part of being human is having emotions. Because of that, we can't untangle them from logic and critical thinking entirely, but we do need to be mindful of when our emotions cloud our judgement. If we always made decisions based solely on emotion, we'd have a lot of worldly problems right now... and perhaps a few more country songs about smashed cars.

As good as an emotional decision might feel in the moment, it often gets us later.

Emotional bias refers to making an emotional decision rather than just considering your emotions along with the facts.

When we make decisions based on our emotions, we often do so quickly. We don't consider other options, the draws and drawbacks, or anything else that would be a part of the critical thinking process. We also don't take the time to learn from these decisions. Often when decisions are made in the heat of the moment, it takes a person a moment to realize what the outcome of that decision even is. We either refuse to acknowledge that the decision might have been a bad one, or we cringe when we think of the event, and we refuse to consider it.

Rather than making decisions based on emotion, it's better to consider your emotions along with the draws and drawbacks of each option for your decision. This way, you weigh the logic behind each decision, while still taking how you feel into account.

The most logical decision may not be the best one for you, but letting our emotions rule our choices can get us into some tricky spots.

Cognitive Bias

Cognitive bias refers to various thought patterns that cloud our decision-making capabilities. These are tough to avoid since the structure of our brain is often built around them, but with some concentrated effort, you can do it.

The first key is to be aware of the biases that you're up against.

First, what bias did we see in Emily's story, other than social bias?

Confirmation Bias

First, there might be some evidence of confirmation bias.

Emily's teacher believes that students who are going through a rough patch in their home lives are more likely to cheat. As Emily starts going through this time in her life, he may have even been on the lookout for a sudden increase in performance or other evidence of academic dishonesty. Seeing the paper gave him further evidence for his view, and even though he was presented with other evidence (the tutor Emily got) he chose to ignore that evidence until it made its way to the principal. Confirmation bias refers to looking only at the information that supports your opinion and ignoring, sometimes viciously, any evidence that stands against it (MasterClass, 2021).

Fundamental Attribution Error

The second cognitive bias that the teacher exhibits is the fundamental attribution error. This might be the most glaringly obvious of his cognitive biases. The fundamental attribution error means that we have attributed certain characteristics of a group onto a single person (MasterClass, 2021). Essentially, we've participated in stereotyping.

When we act on stereotypes, we group a lot of potentially incorrect facts together with little evidence and we miss a lot of the big picture.

Anchoring Bias

There is one more bias that her teacher could be accused of

committing and that's the anchoring bias. When we use this bias, we start out with a judgment or fact that we completely believe in, and we actively rework all the information that we have to support this one fact (MasterClass, 2021).

This one is commonly seen in party-based politics. A member of a specific party may look up to one candidate, even if they hold a lot of the opposing party's views. Similarly, they might choose to overlook a candidate in the opposite party, even if that candidate seems like they would support a lot of their views.

Beyond these, there are many other biases to consider.

Mood Biases

Optimism and Pessimism biases refer to our moon's influence on our thinking and decisions (MasterClass, 2021). When we are in a good mood, we tend to overestimate the day. We make decisions and expect a positive outcome. On the other hand, when we are in a bad mood, we might make decisions with a negative outcome in mind.

Dunning Kruger Effect

The Dunning Kruger effect is a bias rooted in a lack of understanding of a certain topic (MasterClass, 2021).

Now, this may come as a shock, but I am not an astronaut. As such, I've never been inside a spaceship let alone flown one (I have seen one, but that was in the safety of a museum). If you were to ask me, I would equate flying a spaceship to driving a car or at best, flying an airplane (I'm not a pilot either). Needless to say, it's a lot more complicated. If I started studying it, I would likely feel like I understand less about flying a spaceship than I did before I started. When we think we're understanding less about a subject, we are more likely to give up our studies.

Self-Serving Bias

This bias refers to how we view situations where our performance should have affected the result. If the result is what we wanted, we're going to celebrate and pat ourselves on the back for the hard work. On the other hand, if the result isn't what we were hoping for then we are more likely to blame an outside source (MasterClass, 2021). For example, if your mother tries a new recipe and it turns out really well, she's likely to congratulate her own skills in creating the dish. However, if it isn't actually that great, she's more likely to blame the recipe as the reason for the failure. If the self-serving bias is used continuously, we will be too busy making excuses for our mistakes and we won't actually fix them.

Hindsight Bias

Finally, let's talk about hindsight bias. You've probably heard the saying that hindsight isn't always 20/20, and that's true. This bias happens when a person thinks they have foreseen an event that happened. In reality, they've likely anticipated a few different outcomes, one of which ended up being correct (MasterClass, 2021). The danger of this bias is that we start to think we can predict the future, or we expect that the outcome we want is the one we're going to get. This will likely turn into an issue sooner rather than later when we don't prepare ourselves for the negative outcome to happen.

These biases come from weak points in our overall thought process. Now that you are aware of them, you can start working on your own, and finding it in others' thought processes.

Bias isn't the only thing that will get in the way of critical thinking. Logical fallacies can also ruin an argument.

Logical Fallacies

A person never means to have a weak point in their argument, but all too often logical fallacies are committed intentionally, even if the person doesn't immediately realize that is what they are doing. When they aren't spotted, people will rally around the person using them. When they are, an entire argument can unravel in seconds. You may have accidentally used a logical fallacy in an argument with your parents, only for them to spot it right away.

When you know what different fallacies are out there, not only will you be able to avoid them but when it comes to being in a disagreement with parents, teachers, and other authority figures, you will be able to point out their use of them.

Appeal to Ignorance

An appeal to ignorance states that because we don't have evidence, then the information must be whatever we want it to be (TBS Staff, 2022). The use of this argument varies, and in your home, you might have heard it as "I understand more about this subject because I've lived longer." They are using the fact that you don't have the information yet to prove that they are right.

This is a logical fallacy because it relies on a lack of knowledge to work. To disprove the point the person is making, you can simply find the answers or point out that a lack of evidence means that it's not true until proven otherwise.

Appeal to Hypocrisy

Have you ever seen a relationship where one person accuses their partner of cheating, and it is later revealed that they had been the ones doing so? That's an appeal to hypocrisy. This logical fallacy refers to making an allegation against another person for doing something that the accuser is guilty of in order for the accuser to direct the attention away from their actions (TBS Staff, 2022). Once the allegation is in the air, it won't be long before someone takes a look at the skeletons in the accuser's closet. Because of what they've said, people will already know what to look for.

If this logical fallacy is ever used against you, you can refute it by asking for the direct proof they have that you've committed it.

Bandwagon Fallacy

You might not have heard of this phrase, but have you heard the term mob mentality? This fallacy refers to the belief that because everyone agrees with something, you should too (TBS Staff, 2022). If you are in a group and they are all agreeing with something, you are more likely to agree too. But if you were on your own, you might not have made the same decision.

Ad Hominem

The first presidential election where I was old enough to understand what was going on (well, mostly) was in 2016. The candidates for that year were both unique, with one being a woman and the other having never held public office before. What I don't remember is seeing each person take a moment and talk about their stance. What I do remember is the two presidential nominees verbally attacking each other–a lot. They spent most of their time pointing to traits that didn't really matter to a presidency, making them both guilty of the ad hominem fallacy.

The ad hominem fallacy is often used when we have nothing else to say to our opponent and we resort to verbally lashing out at them (TBS Staff, 2022). It's important to note that in order for the ad hominem fallacy to have been committed, the point that the person has made can't relate to the argument in any way.

If you have ever raised a good point with your parents and gotten "I don't like your tone" as a response, then that is an ad hominem.

Circular Arguments

I remember sitting in a youth group one day and a guest pastor used the phrase "I know god exists because the bible says god is real." While I understand where he was trying to go, the phrase felt wrong to me and that was because it contained a circular argument. A circular argument is when you try to prove your point using that same point as evidence (TBS Staff, 2022). You didn't add any new information to the statement.

When using critical thinking, whether it's in a debate or a research project, you need to be able to save solid points to back up your conclusion. The guest pastor, for example, could have pointed to miracles that have happened after prayer to prove his point.

Straw Man

A straw man fallacy happens when one or both parties choose the weakest point of, or entirely misguide their audience about an argument (TBS Staff, 2022). For example, in one of many squabbles between my siblings, one sibling told the other that they were full of themselves–the other sibling responded with "yeah, but at least I'm faster and stronger than you." This was certainly a strawman fallacy (and in my opinion it proved a point).

False Dilemma

A false dilemma happens when a fake two-option scenario is created in a situation with a wide variety of potential outcomes (TBS Staff, 2022).

One example is the belief that you have to get an A in every class, or you will fail. There are many options in between that do not equal failure, so this statement is faulty. If you feel like you're being led into one of these, think about the situation yourself and see if the two polar opposite options you've been given are really all that you have.

Red Herring

This is an unusual name for a logic issue, but it makes sense once you realize what it means. Imagine seeing a literal red herring. No matter where you are or what you are doing, you are likely to get distracted and watch the herring float by instead.

In this fallacy, the red herring is figurative, but it has the same effect. It's something in the conversation that causes your focus to wander from the original topic (TBS Staff, 2022).

Red herrings aren't always committed maliciously. You might even accidentally do it to yourself. If you notice one has been successfully pulled on you, just pause and move back to the original topic, bringing the other person with you.

Equivocation

Equivocations can either be really funny, or a very dirty way to confuse people. This fallacy is when a word is thrown into the conversation in order to throw people off (TBS Staff, 2022). At best, it's done by a comedian who is trying to make you laugh. At worst, it's done intentionally by a politician.

For example, when talking about illegal immigration the president at the time, Donald Trump, said this: "You're looking at people that come in, in many cases, in some cases with evil intentions. I don't want that. They're ISIS(2017)."

The equivocation comes in twice. First, when he contradicts himself (saying many cases and in some cases within the same sentence) and second when talking about ISIS, a Middle Eastern terrorist organization, while he's actively working on the Mexican border wall.

Appeal to Authority

In Emily's story, we witnessed an appeal to authority when she was talking to the principal. She referenced the school board in her cheating case, even though they don't have specific authority to do anything about the case of a single student.

An appeal to authority is an inappropriate use of a person or organization's authority, be it an authority of power or an intellectual authority (TBS Staff, 2022). This can happen when we, like Emily, name someone who has more power but can't control the situation, or when we use someone's credentials to back up a claim they aren't qualified to make. For instance, The

CDC can comment on anything related to the medical field, but they probably shouldn't be sourced for climate change.

Hasty Generalization

In Chapter 1, I mentioned handling snakes as a child. Based on that experience, I might say that all snakes are okay with being picked up, but the specific logical fallacy I would be making there is a hasty generalization. Rather than pulling from facts and research, I am using a few specific examples based on my personal experience (TBS Staff, 2022).

Emily's teacher is also doing this. He's pulling examples from other students to explain why he's accusing her of cheating.

Causal Fallacy

Causal fallacies misrepresent a cause-and-effect relationship between one event and another (TBS Staff, 2022). In other words, when you say that one event has caused a different event when there is little to no connection between the two, you have committed a causal fallacy. They can be completely unrelated, like saying that lasers cause climate change, or they can also just be missing a link. For example, if Emily's teacher were to say that the divorce caused her to cheat, he'd be committing this fallacy. If she had cheated, the cause-and-effect relationship would look more like the divorce causing emotional strain, which caused her grades to slip, which caused the cheating.

Appeal to Pity

Emily used this one as well, and she did so successfully. When she went to the principal, she made a point of noting that the divorce with her parents had already brought her enough stress.

An appeal to pity is making use of an unfortunate situation to extract an emotional response that detracts from the original argument (TBS Staff, 2022). While an appeal to pity isn't always as malicious as other logical fallacies, it does detract from the logic of an argument.

There are times when an appeal to pity can be considered a valid point, especially considering that being human means that we don't always deal with logical situations, but even in these cases, it does detract from a logical argument. For example, when she first ran, House Representative Alexandria Ocasio-Cortez used an "I'm just like you" strategy as a part of her campaign. While this point isn't invalid, it does stand out a bit more than some of her logically based points.

Sunk Cost Fallacy

The sunk cost fallacy is one that we are more likely to commit against ourselves as opposed to anyone else.

When you have already put in a lot of time and energy into something, you don't want to give it up. If we do, then all of that time will be wasted. Unfortunately, the continued cost is likely to overshadow the benefits (Thompson, 2022). If we realize this and still continue, we are committing the sunk cost fallacy.

Slippery Slope

If any of my friends out there have anxiety, you will absolutely recognize this as an everyday pattern. A slippery slope is using one event to predict a chain of events, often the ones that are the worst-case scenario (TBS Staff, 2022). Our mind plays this trick on us... and so do people with power.

If you ever find yourself stuck in this loop, then pause for a breath and remind yourself that one bad thing does not determine a chain of events.

How to Recognize and Avoid Biases and Logical Fallacies

You've probably heard the phrase that "knowing something is

half the battle" and when it comes to logical issues in critical thinking, it really is. Now that you know what to look for, you can easily spot errors in logic and thinking whether you're watching a political candidate give a speech or you are locked in a debate of your own. I would recommend brushing up on these terms every so often in order to keep them fresh in your mind (maybe at least once a year), but now that you've been introduced to them, they will never fully leave your mind. Now it's time to put this into action. Try studying your mind for any sign of bias. They are often ingrained in our brain, but you now have the right tools to find them.

Now it's time to practice. For this, you can go to debates in your school when they are hosted. Another thing that I like to do is look at political sources. You can find debates and speeches that go back years. Additionally, try going to local events hosted by the politicians in your cities and see what you can find there. Not only is this a good way to figure out how to spot logical errors, but it can help you prepare to vote later. It's also a lot of fun to be able to call out logical mistakes in someone's performance.

Finally, if you know that you might be heading into a debate, try to clear your mind. Make a note of any bias that might get you or any logical fallacy that you're prone to and be ready.

Logical fallacies aren't always committed verbally. All too often they happen on paper where they can be harder to spot.

CHAPTER 3

Inspecting Your Sources

The first report I had to write happened to be during fifth grade. It was at this moment that source citations were first introduced.

Why are they so important? Why is it that they are so stressful?

To help you understand why your teachers make such a big deal about them, here is a scenario that might become familiar to you soon.

As a freshman in college, James was enjoying a lot of things. One of them was freedom. His free time was his to do with what he wished. His class professors didn't have rules about attendance or bathroom breaks. There wasn't a lot of pestering regarding his assignments either. His first college assignment was a simple sheet of paper that detailed a small report he needed to write. James felt like he had no trouble cranking it out. He knew he'd written the paper really well, but when he got it back, his grade was well below what he was expecting. A good portion of the paper had also been outlined in red. When he took a look at the comments, he was stunned.

His teacher had highlighted most of his citations and criticized them. He highlighted some of his facts and said they were false. He also got points knocked off because he didn't make use of a scholarly journal in his work.

In shock, James took the paper to his teacher's office hours and asked what had happened. He'd written his argument well and the citations were proper, but they weren't the right sources.

What does it mean to have the right sources? How much of a difference can it make?

Evaluating Our Sources

It does turn out that our sources matter a great deal. The more controversial the topic, the deeper you have to dig to find a good source. When college hits, you are likely to go through some steps to evaluate your sources. Let's save some time and go over them now.

Criteria For Your Sources

Every source can be evaluated based on certain criteria. Let's go over them!

Your Author

First of all, can you find the author on the website? Most should list it, but sites that aren't as careful with their facts don't always want to. By not putting an author, there isn't any responsibility for incorrect facts. Now, if a person is worried to put their face on their work, is it safe to use as a source?

Now, this doesn't automatically mean that a website with a listed author is a good one. You can usually double check the credentials of the author. Those who know they are qualified will often add a bio that lists certain achievements that have made them qualified to speak on the topic at hand. Others might require a Google search. This is a good time to check for an incorrect appeal to authority. A person might have some great credentials, but in order for them to matter, they need to apply to what you're writing about.

A final thing to check for is any bias that the author might have. In this case, bias refers to anything that might hurt the author's ability to be more objective. Let's say that an author has written a book on a diet. Their objectivity to write about different diets is now questionable because a book on a specific diet is making them money. Now, some websites do make the authors list anything that might harm their objectivity, but there are several that will not.

Evidence

Once you've checked the author out, you need to know what evidence they have. Depending on their credentials they could have gathered the evidence themselves, or it might be in the form of a citation.

In order to gather the evidence, they will have needed to conduct research on a large population of people. They also would have needed to have someone with them to conduct this research. Be wary if you see that the sample size is really small, or if you notice that the research doesn't have an assistant of any kind. To verify the results of a small sample, you can fact-check it against a similar piece of research.

Now, we have to be fair when it comes to ensuring that there are multiple researchers. Budgets for research can be tight. Many times, the solution to this is to get college students involved. There might be an unpaid internship and the college student is gaining experience. They might be listed as an author, but they also might not be. There are times when the most a college student has is one line note in the document that lists their contributions.

If you aren't sure, you can always contact the author to see.

Now, sometimes an author won't do their own research. Instead, they will rely on the things that others have done. In this case, they should be citing their sources. You can fact-check these sources (and sometimes, fact-check the sources of these sources) in order to make sure that the information isn't being spun in a certain way for you.

Objectivity

Once you've checked your author and your facts, it's time to check for objectivity. Try to scout out any opinion statements that the author has made and make sure that what you are using is a truly unbiased source. You should also check for this when you are fact-checking. Many people might only mention part of a study that goes along with what they are saying when there is a part of the study that contradicts their point.

Funding

This helps provide a clue as to how objective the paper really is. In order to ensure that what you are consuming is truly neutral, it's best to be aware of where a study's funding comes from. If it comes from a company that would benefit from a certain result, then it's time to go over the source with a fine-tooth comb. If the result seems skewed, then you know that it might not be a good source. For example, let's say that research of a certain vaccine is funded by the company that makes it. The company might pick and choose in order to achieve a 100% success rate (or close to it) even though the successful number sits lower.

Check for Fallacies

The final thing to do to evaluate a source is to check it over for any sign of bias or a logical fallacy. When these are present in any paper, it's a sign that the author is trying to persuade you in some way, and it often means that research was cherry picked or done incorrectly.

To summarize, the best sources will have an author that is an expert in the topic and research that is either heavily cited or done by the author and another person. It will be free of any bias, whether that comes from the funding or the author itself, and it will be free of any logical fallacies.

Now, realistically, perfect sources are few and far between. You can have some give in most areas and still have a pretty good source. An author may not be an expert, but they can still do a lot of research and cover the topic well. In certain cases, like in the medical field, it's hard to find bias-free work because medical companies have to do tests on their treatment methods, and these often have to be self-funded. The one area you can't give any leeway to is having good evidence. If the evidence isn't that great or it can't be backed up, then we don't have a good source on our hands.

When you're just using a regular search engine, these sources don't come easily. To find them, we have to use some different strategies.

Locating Reliable Resources

With us now having gone over the various ways to ensure that your sources are good ones, let's start talking about where these good sources might be located.

Internet Searches

You can technically find them with a Google search, but it's harder. You're going to want to double check the credibility of the website you found the source on along with the source itself. There are several quality sites that you can find on Google that will give you the information at no cost. These can be good sites for arguments and research papers.

Museum Sites

If you are looking at a specific topic that might have a following, try a museum website. Several sites keep information about their exhibits, and they might include facts about them on the site too. The tricky part about museum websites is that because they want you to pay and see the exhibits, they may not contain all the helpful information that the museum has for what you're trying to research.

In this instance, you have a few natural qualities that will help you. Many people don't think to reach out to get more information and the younger a person gets, the truer this becomes. Because of this, if you were to reach out, you have a solid shot of getting an informative response.

Try to find the museum director, someone who works for the exhibit, or even someone who helped to create the exhibit. There might be a way to use the website to send a message or, in some cases, someone has left a contact email. Reach out and let them know you are a student who has some questions for a report. If they respond, send those questions. You can often find out some great information this way.

News

There are often accusations out there that the news is untrustworthy, and the news itself can have some bias. That being said, news stories are required to be truthful. If they are not, newspapers can end up in serious legal trouble. Truthful doesn't mean unbiased, but you now have the tools to scan for that bias.

The news can often be a great way to get firsthand information on something. It's also a great place to gather other sources for your topic, as a news article will have documented its sources.

Trustworthy Sites

Beyond museums and the news, there are a few other places that you can go to find information regarding your research.

The thing that all of these have in common is that they receive federal funding. Because of this, they are held to a certain standard and the information that comes out must be truthful if they don't want to risk losing funding.

Some of these sites include the Center for Disease Control (CDC), The Food and Drug Administration (FDA), the United States Department of Agriculture (myplate.gov), and the World Health Organization (WHO). You can use these sites as sources themself, but you can also use this site to find sources for your work by taking a look at what these sites have used.

Oftentimes, especially as you enter college, professors will ask you to dive into deeper research.

Scholarly Articles

Articles go beyond even some of the best website sources. The author for these is an expert in their field (or at least, studying rigorously to become one) and they have done the research themselves. The article is a means to tell the world about their work. Now, not every article is perfect. An expert can still be biased, and the research done could have some shady funding, but articles go through a rigorous review process before they can be published and as a part of it these issues are revealed. It's also often required for an author to reveal where they got their funding from in an article and if they have any known bias there is often a section toward the bottom to discuss it. Articles are also often written by more than one author, so that can be an added layer of protection to stop biased information.

To find scholarly articles, you're going to want to use some databases rather than doing a Google search.

One place to look is Google Scholar. To find this, you can simply type it into your Google search bar, and it should come right up. Google Scholar will look through all the public journals and you can find what you're looking for pretty quickly. If you are having trouble finding what you need with the first set of keywords that you've typed in, it will often suggest other ideas to you so that you have a better chance of finding the right source. One of the struggles with Google Scholar, that I have found at least, is that it doesn't have any way to filter out sources that will require you to pay money. Many articles do cost money, and the priciest one I saw was about $150. The reasons behind this are that these are usually published in scientific journals which require a subscription, and that in order to continue doing research, the authors need additional funding. These are good reasons, but as you might already know, when we are in high school and later college, it isn't feasible to pay for every article that we need.

To avoid this, there are some other databases that we can search that will contain free articles.

One of the biggest is the National Center for Biotechnology Information or NCBI. This database has been created by the National Institute of Health (NIH) as a go to source for anything with even the slightest relation to the medical field. I found this gem while studying psychology, and there are numerous reports for mental and physical health, nutrition, technology, history, and so much more. Not every article is free, but this source will sort through them for you if you ask it to.

There are other databases like this (such as History.com and PubMed.gov) and while they are smaller, you can still find some great things.

Another thing you can do, especially if you know that you're going to have to do a lot of research on a particular topic, is to subscribe to a journal for that topic. This way you are paying a small monthly fee to get access to all the articles you would need to do your research.

Fact-Checking

Whether you're using a source from Google, or you are getting an article, it's good to fact-check what's being said.

To fact-check, you're going to want to start out with their references list. If it's a website from Google, it will likely have a reference sheet at the end. If not—that could be a red flag. Articles will often have a reference list at the bottom as well, except in the cases where the research was too unique to have prior sources.

When you access their sources, the most obvious thing to check for is making sure that the information on the website is also in the sources. Going beyond that, we also need to make sure that the sources say the same thing that the webpage says. For example, the webpage may say "this diet has helped 75% of its users achieve their goal" when the source information says "25% of those who tried this diet found that they weren't losing weight and it was harming their body."

While the webpage you are sourcing may not entirely be lying, it is certainly twisting the facts, something we wouldn't have seen without fact-checking.

A final step with fact-checking is to check other sources to make sure that everything lines up. If you notice that all sources are saying the same thing, then we have good information! However, if the source you found is saying one thing but all the sources you are trying to use to confirm it are saying another, then something might be wrong.

Fact-checking might seem like a lot of work. Honestly, it is a lot of work, but it's worth every second. When we go through this process, we're making sure that our facts are backed up and they are actually true. If you're writing a paper, there is a good chance that your teacher will fact-check your paper, especially if they assigned the topic. Having fact-checked it already, you can avoid getting points taken off of your grade.

If you're getting ready for a discussion or an argument, then fact-checking is essential. The other person may have also done their homework and if they have the up-to-date facts and you don't, it could be embarrassing.

Experts

Remember when we talked about finding people to email who work for museums? That doesn't just apply to museums.

It can be nerve wracking to send an email or make a phone call to a field expert. That's why many people don't do it. Funnily enough, this is also why you have a good shot of getting a response if you try this.

Experts aren't just writing papers or webpages about the material you're trying to learn. They are out there sourcing it and experiencing everything firsthand. They may even have made new discoveries in this topic. The thing you are trying to learn about now is something that they are likely to be passionate about. You also have an additional advantage: You're a teenager and you want to learn. I know that doesn't sound like much, but for many who are passionate about what they are doing, having a young audience member that wants to learn is like Christmas morning.

These are the main reasons why I recommend reaching out to these individuals. To find who you might be looking for, check museum and archive sites. Go to the library and ask the librarians what they know (they really do carry a lot of secrets). Check college and university websites and see if you can find professors that teach what you want to learn (since they have already made a career of teaching, they will often be happy to share with you what they know).

Send an initial email to introduce yourself and let them know what you're looking for. Then, once they respond, send your questions. Be willing to take away any information you can.

First-person accounts are often the best sources if you are willing to get them.

All the researching, sourcing, fact-checking, and even the steps for reaching out are worth something. A major part of critical thinking is making sure that we have the right facts to think with. If we don't, not only are there going to be flaws in our thought process, but we are more than likely to find someone who does have the correct facts eventually. When that happens, we put our credibility at risk.

Finding incorrect information also gives you power. When you are able to see past an original source, you've proven yourself to be smarter than the person who wrote it. Having the correct facts also gives you a leg up in every discussion.

You're well on your way to teaching your brain to question everything before it solidifies in your mind as a fact. Sometimes we need to dig deeper and start asking some questions.

Chapter 4

Asking the Right Questions

Walk through this scenario with me for a moment.

You are stressed, maybe even anxious. Last week, you took a math test, and it was one of the most difficult tests you've ever taken. Your teacher is strict and you're almost certain they made the test difficult on purpose because your class has been slower to grasp things than their other class. Your teacher passed back the exams today and even though you are normally a great student, you failed the exam.

Your teacher has given you a heads up that they've emailed everyone's parents to complain about your class not paying any attention. Since your parents are strict, you know that it isn't going to be a fine conversation.

Sure enough, when you get home, your mom is waiting. She is ready to ground you and interrogate as to why you aren't paying attention.

Critical thinking and asking the right questions can save you now. I have been in this position before (more often in college than high school) and here is what I have learned to ask.

The first thing you ask is if this behavior matches up with your normal routine. If all of your other teachers don't have a complaint, and your grades in their class aren't any different from this class, then why did this teacher say something?

Second, what was it that made this test so hard?

Third, what is the average grade for this teacher? Is it usually this hard?

You can investigate these questions and when you find your answers you've potentially stopped yourself from getting grounded, and you may have stopped your teacher from giving out unfair grades.

Now, imagine if you hadn't asked these questions. What would have happened then?

Why Questions Are Important

A key component of critical thinking is ensuring that we are questioning everything. We don't accept facts at face value, even if the fact came from a trusted source.

When you are doing research for things like a paper or a debate, you question things by reaching out to multiple experts and fact-checking your sources. When we can't research or fact-check, such as in cases like an angry math teacher, we still have our questions.

Ask questions that dig deeper into the issue. Ask the ones that make people uncomfortable. If your instincts are telling you to ask a question, do it! There isn't much to lose when you ask good questions. After all, in the example above, you have already failed the test, so what else could really happen?

Asking Effective Questions That Get to The Bottom of Things

The questions we ask as a part of our critical thinking process aren't just there to give us simple answers. We ask them in order to get to the bottom of something. For that, we do need to make some changes in how we question things.

Asking Open-Ended Questions

First, you want to make sure that your first set of questions is always open-ended. Open-ended questions are ones that require more than a one-word answer. In fact, they may require as much as a paragraph to be fully answered.

These questions get you more information and they make the source of that information have to dig deeper and be honest about their answers.

For example, it may be hard for you to go to your teacher and ask questions, but if your parent went in and asked how exactly you were being disruptive, the teacher would have to give a clear response. To do so she would either have to think and be specific or potentially admit that your behavior isn't that crazy.

Asking Clarifying Questions

Clarifying questions also have a fair bit of power. They are often needed for open-ended questions. Once you have asked your open-ended question, either write down or make a mental note of any clarifying questions that you would need to ask. These can tie up some loose ends that the open-ended questions created.

Asking Probing Questions

Open-ended questions have a good chance of catching a source off guard and giving you some real answers. Sometimes, however, the person is more than prepared for the questions you're about to ask. The responses seem guarded, and they give away as little information as they possibly can. If they are feeling bold, they might even try to move on before the question is fully answered. If that's the case, it's time to start asking probing questions. They do bear some semblance to clarifying questions and you might be making them on the fly, but your goal is to use these questions to dig into something.

It is almost like you're leading an interrogation, even if the topics you're discussing aren't related to crime.

Have Goals

Your goals can help keep you from getting sidetracked in the discussion. When you're forming open-ended questions, and then clarifying and probing them, you risk getting sucked into a rabbit hole of one specific conversation pattern rather than dealing with the issue you initially set out to solve. If you have someone who is trying to avoid the topic you want to discuss, then you are at even greater risk.

To avoid this, set some goals at the beginning of your conversation. What is it that you hope to solve with this conversation? What answers are you looking for?

Keep Your Ears Open

When we are engaging in critical thinking, it's important that we do two things. First, we don't want to reveal everything we are thinking in the first breath. Keeping some things to yourself, especially if we aren't 100% certain of something, can help us make sure that we have all the facts before we reach our conclusion.

The other thing we need to make sure of is that we listen just as much, if not more, than we talk.

As we start developing the critical thought process in our minds, we need to make sure that a healthy respect for our conversation partner is coming with it. If we write the other person off too early, we might miss some good points that they have. They may also not be revealing all that they know right away, but the more we listen, the more they will say.

When it's your turn to speak, consider their words before you add your own.

Impose Multi Directional Thinking

When you are considering an issue, whether it's simple or complex, don't get stuck in one directional thinking. This means that you're considering only one issue. We talked about this a bit in critical thinking when it comes to problem solving. Whether it's problem solving, research, or entering a debate, we need to be ready for every possibility, no matter how unlikely.

If you don't ask questions, you won't get any further than you are right now. Keep that in mind.

Practice

Effective questioning becomes better with some practice.

Write Open-Ended Questions

One thing you can do is practice writing open-ended questions. Remember, these kinds of questions will take about a paragraph to respond to, but they can be hard to come up with on the fly if you aren't used to them.

Make a Habit of Listening First

Life can sometimes give us too many opportunities to listen, especially when we are in our teens. Take every one of them.

Practice by listening to what others have to say, even if you disagree. When they have finished what they are saying, process it and decide what the best response will be before you speak.

Not only does this help you to appear more mature and in control, but with time it will also become more natural... and really helpful for getting out of trouble in certain situations.

Join Debates

Debate teams regularly practice critical thinking skills even if they don't realize it. By joining, you not only get a chance to practice effective questioning, but you can also practice other critical thinking skill sets.

Join a School Newspaper

When you join your school newspaper, you are likely to have to conduct interviews for stories.

Start with the open-ended questions. Then, use your clarifying and probing questions as needed.

Start Papers With Questions

When it's time to do research, you can start with open-ended questions that you intend to answer.

Your goal will likely already be set thanks to the assignment. Using it, you can create your open-ended questions and create clarifying questions based on what you find. Before you know it, you will have all the information needed to write your paper.

Questions play a key role in analyzing arguments, which is what we are going to talk about next!

Chapter 5

Analyzing Arguments

Critical thinking is often most helpful when it comes to taking a look at arguments and picking them apart. Not every argument is a bad an unethical one, but many of them contain logical fallacies and when it comes to arguments with authority figures like parents and teachers, you'll have a hard time getting them to listen if you don't know what you're doing.

Let's go back to talking to your parents about the math test. In Chapter 4 we discussed an unfair test and an angry teacher. Your teacher accused you and the rest of the class of having been fooling around and not paying attention, and they are saying that's why everyone did poorly. Your parent is angry at you after having got this note, but you have a few ways you can pick this argument apart.

Steps For Analyzing An Argument

Identify the Main Claim

First off, what is the main claim for the argument? Every argument is trying to prove one thing. This claim should be able to be formed into a statement, and it can be a fact or an opinion as long as there is evidence to back it up.

In our example above, your teacher is trying to prove that the class failed the test because they had been messing around instead of paying attention.

Identify the Supporting Evidence

Once you have the claim you are investigating narrowed down, it's time to look at the evidence there is to support it. Some evidence might be readily available to you, but for other evidence, you might need to dig.

Now, if you think about it, the only evidence we have on hand for this situation is your test. Also, depending on the computer program your school uses, you might be able to see the average, high, and low scores of the tests. You can add this evidence if it's available.

Beyond this, what other evidence do you think you can get? For arguments that you are trying to analyze, write down a list of things that can act as evidence for this claim. One example in this current argument is the test scores of other students and your past work for this teacher.

Evaluating the Evidence

Once you have the evidence, evaluate each piece against the claim, then evaluate the evidence as a whole.

Let's look at each piece of evidence, and how it relates to the claim.

First, you know that you've been paying attention in your teacher's class. However, you can't really prove that to your parents, so that is more of a personal piece of evidence. When we evaluate this piece of evidence against the claim (that the low-test scores were due to people not paying attention), it doesn't stick very well.

The next piece of evidence we have is your own failing test score. Well, low test scores are in the claim. It can't be used as evidence because it commits a logical fallacy. To use a claim as evidence is a circular argument. Based on that, this doesn't hold up very well either.

This also applies to your classmates' test scores. None of that can be used to prove your teacher's claim.

So, what about the scores of those who take the same class, but not in the same period you do? Your teacher's claim only applies to your class as far as you know, so other classes' scores do qualify as evidence. For the sake of this argument, let's say that those scores are only slightly higher than your classes scores were. Were they all messing around too, or is it something else?

Finally, there is your coursework for this class. We established in Chapter 4 that you are generally a good student with As in most of your classes. Until now, this class hadn't been an exception. You go through your work, and you notice something else. A lot of the problems on your test aren't covered in the work you've done so far. This is concrete evidence that you can give to your parents. With that also being said, this evidence isn't really measuring up to the claim either.

So, let's evaluate this argument as a whole. None of the evidence seems to be foolproof. Some of it contains logical fallacies. Overall, there might be other arguments that provide a better explanation.

Consider Counter Arguments

Now, at this point, we have had an in-depth look at the argument the teacher created for all the evidence you could find that relates to the issue. We are at a point where you would consider counter arguments. I always recommend doing this step, even if the original argument does seem completely valid. Why? Well, remember when the Earth was believed to be flat? If we don't consider all the possibilities, we are nearly certain to miss something.

So, what other possibilities can you think of that might pertain to this situation?

Here are a few that come to mind. Remember, write down anything you can think of, even if it seems a little out of the ordinary.

- Your teacher doesn't like your class.

- Your teacher wants everyone to fail.

- You didn't pass because there was material on there your teacher didn't cover.

- Your teacher is mad at a select few individuals and she's taking it out on the whole class.

- Your teacher is a government agent secretly testing all the students to find out how much they can stand.

So, now that we have a few things, we need to examine the

evidence for each possibility. For some, the evidence you've already collected will likely do. For others, you might need a few additional pieces.

First, let's examine your teacher for not liking your class. You know from talking to others who have that teacher that the test scores they got were either the same or slightly higher than your class. That piece of evidence can disprove this theory (at least as the reason why your class failed).

Next, does your teacher want everyone to fail? For this, we need additional pieces of evidence. It's no secret that school is based on performance, and it's not uncommon for a school's funding to get cut if students aren't doing well. Because of this, it would be counterintuitive for your teacher to want everyone to fail.

Now, our third possibility is that there was material on the test that the teacher didn't cover. As a part of our previous evidence, you compared the test to your homework, and you noticed that a lot of the problems on the test weren't covered in the homework. This supports this theory.

Up next is the assumption that your teacher is mad at a few individuals and she's taking it out on the class. What evidence is there for this? She did complain about the entire class. You might need to gather some evidence for this, but to do that, you can simply sit and see what others are doing during class.

Finally, there is the theory that your teacher is secretly an agent testing everyone to see how long it takes them to snap. We can't specifically find evidence against this, so far there isn't any evidence for it. Until there is, we'd need to let this theory go.

Now that we have considered all the possibilities, we can see that some arguments do come out being more logically sound than others. What do you think that means?

Determining an Argument's Validity

At this point, we have reviewed what the argument is. We have looked at all the evidence and its validity. We have also discussed any other options there might have been as an explanation.

Now, we must determine whether or not this argument is valid. We can do so with a few simple tests.

Logical Soundness Test

The logical soundness test breaks up an argument into a series of statements. The conclusion is the end result, and the premises are the statements we need to back it up. For an argument to be sound, all the premises and the conclusion need to be verifiably true. Take a look.

Major premise: All disruptive students fail the test.

Minor premise: You did not pay attention in class.

Conclusion: You failed the test.

This argument can only be logically sound if both premises are correct in a way that leads the conclusion to be correct.

Evidence: Is it Sufficient and Relevant

Let's think back to the evidence that we have right now. Is it all relevant? In other words, does it all connect to the argument? Are these premises supported?

We can safely say that the evidence was relevant and connected.

A piece of evidence that wasn't relevant might be what the teacher had for lunch that day.

Now, what about sufficient? One thing we didn't cover was the attitude of the class from your perspective, which would be a pretty big part of the argument. Without having that evidence, the argument isn't sufficient.

Are There Any Logical Fallacies

The final thing to do is to pick apart the argument and simply aim to locate as many logical fallacies as you can. We did manage to locate a few in our story, most notably the circular argument.

So, with all of this laid out, what do you think? Is the argument logically sound?

Personally, I don't think so. You definitely have a case here to avoid getting grounded.

While many of our stories have covered real work scenarios, we must ask ourselves a question. When, in the real world, should I be using my critical thinking?

CHAPTER 6

Applying Critical Thinking to Real World Situations

So, to answer the question from the previous chapter, you should use your critical thinking skills often, but especially in the areas we are about to discuss. As it stands, these are often the areas that need you to apply critical thinking.

When we do, we can spot lies and misinformation and walk away from things with a better-informed mind. When we don't, we might take away false information that can really impact us down the line. Yes, I do realize that sounds dramatic, but hear me out.

Imagine you are scrolling through TikTok, and you come across one of your favorite health creators on the app. They mention that losing weight is easy. You just need to have a calorie deficit. They then recommend a training program designed by another company that has you eating 1,200 calories a day, cutting about 800 from your usual diet. The influencer mentions that several celebrities do it for roles and that it works well for them, so you should, of course, totally try it.

It's dangerous. The 1,200-calorie diet is not enough to sustain you, especially if you ever leave the house to do things (Kubala, 2020). Critical thinking would lead you to this solution relatively quickly, but without it you, might have ended up going on a seriously unsafe diet. This cut has led to low blood sugar, hormonal issues, dizziness and fainting, and more (Kubala, 2020).

To avoid this, we need critical thinking, and here is how to apply it.

Social Media and Online Websites

It seems that everyone, young and old, has forgotten that we should not believe everything we see on social media. People who post on social media have gotten better about making it seem like they're telling the truth, so how do we tell the difference?

Step 1: Evaluate the Source

The first step is always to look at where the information is coming from. Certain sources have better vetting than others.

Scientific journals, for example, have an extensive vetting process to get published. It can take a while (sometimes it really can take years) and if there is any part that doesn't hold up, you can be made to remove it before it gets published. In contrast, social media platforms like Instagram and TikTok don't have any fact-checking protocols. While they might flag blatantly misleading information, most things will fly right under the radar.

When you are looking at your source, ask yourself how well-vetted for misinformation it is. If it isn't well-vetted, be suspicious of any information you get from there.

Step 2: Check the Author

Once you know what the site is like, it's time to check out the author of the content. Again, a scientific journal will have already done some of this for you, but it could still be handy to double check their credentials.

Now, on social media sites, there are plenty of professionals with platforms. Most will boast about their qualifications, and you can usually verify it with a Google search or two. But if they aren't talking about credentials, and you don't have any way to prove that they know what they are talking about, then they may not be able to be trusted.

Now, in place of credentials, a creator can research and present sources. Many do. For this, head to Step 3.

Step 3: Fact-Check It

Once you've dug into the first two steps, it's time to fact-check the information you have. Check other websites and books to see if the information is repeated in other places. Try to find at least one well-vetted site to support the information you found.

Step 4: Double Check For Bias

The author can be credible. The site can be credible. All the facts can line up.

Sadly, that still doesn't mean it's perfect. All of these things could hold true, and the site could still be biased. The author might be emotionally invested for example, or the site might have some biased funding.

If there are facts missing or they are trying to get you to buy something, then there is a good chance that you are being given biased information. As a part of your fact-checking, try to find out what the other side is saying.

Step 5: Double Check the Logic

This final step can ensure that it's logically sound. Check the work for any bias or logical fallacy to ensure that everything is lining up the way it should be!

If all of these steps come together nicely, then you seem to have found a good source of information!

Now, online sources shouldn't contain bias, but media sources are often designed to. Still, they can be useful to us if we know how to break them down.

Media Messages and Advertisements

Advertisements usually exist to sell you s0mething. Media messages exist all around, pushing both fact and fiction. These messages are engineered to get you to think a certain way, so how do we make sure that we don't fall for it?

Step 1: Identify the Bias

With both advertisements and media messages, we need to assume that a bias is already in place. It might be simple, or it might not be.

Start with the company that created the ad. What are they selling?

When it comes to media messages, ask about their platform. Who or what was behind it? What side of the argument is it tied to? A platform can be based around an organization, website, or even a person. To give some examples, the Fox news outlet showcases primarily conservative news. House Member Alexandria Ocasio Cortez has a platform based on immigration and environmental protection.

When we are viewing an advertisement or a message pushed by a platform, we need to view it from that lens. We need to know what they are trying to pursue.

Step 2: Evaluate the Source

Once we know who the company is and what they are trying to sell us, it's time to check them out. What do we know about them?

When checking your source, you want to know how trustworthy they are and how good the product is at doing what it says it will do. You can often Google companies and see if they have faced any major scandals in the last 10 years. If they have, then it's a red flag. You can also find reviews of the company as a whole, and of specific products they generate pretty easily. If you don't find any scandal's and they seem to have a good reputation, plus all of their products rate well, then you have likely found a place that is at least somewhat reliable.

Step 3: Check For Logical Fallacies

This part is pretty simple, but just check over the advertisement and see if you can spot any logical fallacies. A common example is an ad hominem, where they attack their opponents' product rather than dedicate the time to showcasing their own.

Step 4: Fact-Check Their Research

For your final step, you should double check the research the company has done if there is any mentioned. Find out who conducted it and if they were specifically employed by the company. Check on how strong the information is. For example, was the conducted research repeated a few times or was it just one test? If only one test is done, then there is a good chance that the results are unique. They only happened that one time and if we did it again we'd be getting a different result.

In addition to all of this, we should also make sure that the facts are actually correct (while you would think they would be, you can find some nasty surprises by assuming). For example, there are many facts that are subject to interpretation. For instance, if you look at events like January 6th, 2021, when Trump supporters stormed the Capital, everyone has a different opinion. Outlets have called it everything from a peaceful protest that got out of hand to an act of treason. When a fact is subjective, it can hurt an arguments validity.

When it comes to advertisements, we are already starting out with biased information. That being said, ads can teach us about new products, politicians, medications, and other things that will help our lives. We just need to do a little digging to make sure that we are actually getting a useful product.

Making Informed Decisions

Decision making is a bit different from analyzing sources, but it can be very important. Right now, you might be close to finishing high school and that means that you have some big decisions to make. With the right steps, you can make sure that your decision is well-informed.

For this list, we are going to use which college a person might go as an example.

Step 1: Remove the Pressure

Some decisions come with a lot of pressure. Choosing a major and college to go to, for instance, can basically feel like you are planning out your whole life.

In order for us to properly consider our choices, we need to try to mitigate this stress as much as possible. For that, you might want to meditate, draw, bake, or do something that can get your mind off of the issue. When you feel calm and focused, start with Step 2.

Step 2: Lay Out All of Your Facts and Choices

Gather all the facts you can in regard to the decision you have to make and then lay out your choices.

For instance, when you are considering colleges, the first fact you might want to gather is what colleges on your list actually have your major. Based on that, you might be able to narrow down your decision a little bit.

Once you are certain that all the facts have been gathered, you can begin laying out your choices (which, in our example, is each college that you want to go to).

Step 3: Make a List of Pros and Cons for Each Choice

Write down everything that makes each option a good one, and everything that makes each option a bad one.

For example, let's say you've narrowed it down to two colleges, X and Y. For college X you might write that a pro is the low cost, but a con is that the college doesn't have a lot of activities for students. College Y, on the other hand, might have a lot of student life but it could be expensive and far away from home.

Step 4: Consider the Outcomes of Each Choice

Now, what would happen if you made each choice? Try to work through that in your head. One outcome might stick out more than another.

For example, you walk yourself through college X. You have enough saved up that you don't have to get a job. It's close to your parents, which is both good and bad. You can visit, but there is always a chance of them coming in when you least expect it. In the long run, you might have less debt, but you wouldn't have much to do on campus with your free time.

For College Y, it would probably be wise to get a full-time job to help with expenses. Your parents won't be as close, which means it's hard for you to visit them but also hard for them to visit you. There are a lot more opportunities for you to hang out with friends and enjoy life outside of classes here.

Step 5: Make a Decision

Based on the pros and cons, and scenarios you've just run

through, you can now make a decision.

When making your decision, it is often best to think it over yourself without getting others involved, unless you are in real need of their advice. This simply allows you to make the decision on your own terms.

What you decide will depend on what you value.

Step 6: Check In With Yourself

The final thing that you can do is just check in with yourself. Are you happy with the decision you made? If not, what can you revisit? This simple reflection step can save you trouble later on.

Critical thinking can help you identify the facts and separate them from fiction. It can help you analyze ads so that you are certain you are getting good products. It can also help you make some of the best decisions so that you can look back without regrets or worry. Critical thinking is a skill set that will continue to grow if it is properly nourished. In order to do that, there are some exercises in the next chapter. Using them can help you integrate it into your daily life.

Chapter 7

Tips For Improving Critical Thinking Skills

When we become adults, it becomes significantly harder to cultivate skills such as this one. Right now, as a teen, you have the power to do so. Your power does come from the fact that your brain hasn't fully developed. Because of this, it's easy to introduce things such as critical thinking and how to naturally go through its process.

In order to form this as a permanent structure in your brain, we need to start now with a few things that are going to help your brain rise to the occasion. These next tactics are going to be here to do just that.

Read Everything You Can Get Your Hands On

Growing up, you might have been handed a book or two about

bettering yourself or getting friends and making a difference. I know that I still have a certain few of them on my bookshelf. These books are important, but the ones that are about fairytales and romance and adventure are just as important.

Reading expands your mind. It opens you up to new ideas from the mind of another person. You are constantly exposing yourself to new characters and potentially even new worlds.

So, whether you are reading about the power of habit or exploring Middle Earth, you are expanding your mind and filling it with new things!

Movies and TV shows don't have the same power that books do. The characters are already there for you to see and so is the scenery. You are more of a passive observer and less actively engaging with the content.

To practice active reading, start your day off with nonfiction or self-help books (like this one), or possibly some realistic fiction. The reason for this is that it can help get your brain to think peacefully and it can prepare you for the day. When it is closer to your time for bed try looking at the action, adventure, and fantasy parts of your shelf. These will be the things that let your mind enter a world of imagination, and it will give your brain something else to focus on other than the worries of the day. You'll be able to go to bed thinking of the new world you've found yourself in rather than some of the daily worries you face.

Expose Yourself to Diverse Perspectives

Depending on where y0u live, you might have noticed that things have become much more divided and diverse lately. This has a lot of pros, but there are some cons too.

One of the biggest cons that I have seen is that there are many people out there who don't fully understand each side. They find a side that they agree with and then they meet people who also agree with that side. When they all become friends, their opinions can become a product of groupthink. Groupthink happens when a body of people says one thing and even if one or two (or more) people in this collective disagree with what is being said, they will agree with the others to keep the peace. They may also go out of their way to avoid new information about certain issues so that they will have an easier time going along with the rest of the group.

Having friends with shared values can be important, but you never want to find yourself in a situation where you are just agreeing with the group because your own opinion is different. This will corrode your critical thinking powers over time. The primary way to avoid this issue is to continuously expose yourself to diverse perspectives. You can do this by reading, researching, and talking to others who hold different views. You don't have to change what you think, but by taking these steps, you can find holes and logical fallacies within your reasoning. Once you become aware of culturally diverse perspectives in thinking, you can use that to reach out to others and find common ground. Your communication with other groups will improve.

Practice Questioning and Analyzing Arguments

One of the best ways I have found to question the things around me is to study political arguments. Why? There is an abundance of them. Not only do we have footage going back decades, but we also have access to voting records and stances that the opponents had. We can also see just how someone might have persuaded others to vote for them.

You can look at examples from local or national leaders. Use our steps in Chapter 3 to ask questions of the politicians. Even if they are not alive, you can often find the answer on Google or through old newspapers that have been saved online. For example, which president is famous for getting caught spying on his enemies (here's a hint–Watergate)?

Use your argument analysis tools from Chapter 4 too! These tools are going to be great for making sure that you notice even the smallest details.

Being able to look at these old arguments and call out the fallacies that exist within them can be a pretty big deal! When you hear people mentioning policies, both new and old, you will have the knowledge and skills to counter logical fallacies that you have found on the issue.

In the future, this practice will also help you. I know I've brought up voting before and I do mean it when I say that it is the biggest way to ensure that your concerns are being handled in the way you want them to be. The trouble is that not every politician out there is truthful, and being able to pick up on bias and logical fallacies is what's going to help you weed out those that aren't there to help.

Identify Your Own Biases

We can't escape being biased. That's never been the goal. Our best hope has always been to try to figure out what our biases are so that we can avoid acting on them.

When you have a moment, sit down with the list of biases. Go through and try to determine which ones you might have fallen victim to recently. Which ones are you prone to acting on?

Make a game plan that can help you stop acting on these and focus only on the logic of the situation.

For example, let's say that our friend Mira gets into a lot of fights with her boyfriend. She is prone to emotional bias, and she often lets her feelings get in the way of the overall discussion. She knows that her boyfriend will take advantage of this to try to get out of a difficult discussion. She makes a game plan to stop and take a breath if she feels like she's getting riled up. She will go right back to the topic anytime her boyfriend tries to take her focus away from it. And, if she feels that it's needed, she will walk away and come back to the argument later. After all, if she is upset and the argument is carrying away from the original issue, then there isn't any point in continuing it, right?

There's nothing wrong with recognizing that you have biases. It's just a game of making sure that they don't get in your way.

Listen For Logical Fallacies

There are so many logical fallacies out there, and especially as we're getting started with critical thinking, we don't always know what they are.

Now, as you are developing your critical thinking, don't focus too much on learning each logical fallacy and what exactly it means. That can be a long, uphill battle. What we should focus on instead is what they sound like. What does someone really say when they are committing a logical fallacy? How good is your brain at recognizing it?

You don't have to put a name to a logical fallacy for it to be there, you just have to recognize it, especially when it is being used against you.

Practice Active Listening

Imagine, for a moment, that you come home, and your parents are clearly upset with you. They aren't trying to hide it. You think over your actions from the past couple of days. You haven't done anything that would have made them upset. You've kept up on all of your chores and have been on time to school. You've had decent grades. Everything checks out. Your parents come up to you and they immediately talk to you in a stern and upset tone. You aren't sure what's going on, but you can catch that you are being disrespectful and irresponsible.

When this happened in my house, my initial reaction was to immediately jump to my own defense. I needed my family to understand that I didn't do anything wrong and that, for me, this was coming out of nowhere. What happened?

Well, usually they would talk over me, and I was more likely to end up grounded for talking back.

This would be a great time to employ active listening skills. In this situation, let your parents finish. Once they have, you will have collected all the details you need, including the "crime" you are currently being accused of. You can then respond appropriately.

Your active listening skills are a great way to enhance your critical thinking. In a way, you are collecting data by using them. Additionally, by waiting, you've let the other person lay out all of their cards, leaving them with little to respond to you with. If anyone else happens to be watching the discussion, you also appear more respectful (even when you are being accused of a crime you didn't commit).

Self-reflection, exposing ourselves to new ideas, and just being willing to learn are some of the biggest things we can do to enhance our critical thinking. It's thanks to these efforts that we can weed through bias, faulty logic, and lies. In our final chapter, we are going to look at some specific exercises for your critical thinking skills!

CHAPTER 8

Exercises

We don't often notice that we have an opportunity to practice until it's too late. Using these exercises, you can analyze a variety of material to determine how logical and truthful it really is.

Exercise 1: Analyzing a Political Advertisement

If you live in America, you might have caught what happens about every two years. Political ads light up the screen, and we get to wade through them. Now, as you start wondering about voting, it's important to pay attention to who your choices are, but political ads don't always create the best impressions and they don't always give you much more information than you had in the first place. So, how do you know what you're taking away? Are there any ways to tell that you can trust a political candidate?

Step 1: Identify Your Candidate

Because we are working with an advertisement, bias is something we already know is there. Your first goal is to identify the candidate the ad is supporting. Without really knowing this, we can't go much further in our evaluation.

Step 2: Identify Their Opponent

Once we've identified who the supporting candidate is in the ad, we need to look at who they are running against. If they are running against a specific person, the ad will mention this (and it will likely use the most unflattering photo a party could find of that person). Once we have identified who the ad is against, we can inspect what is being said about the opponent. Often, the positions of the opponent will have been tweaked to make them seem as undesirable as possible. When you have identified them, save that information for Step 4.

Step 3: Watch the Ad and Look at What Is Covered

In order to analyze the ad, we must first watch the ad. While you are watching the ad, take note of what the ad is covering. A good political ad will devote most of its time to covering the beliefs and positions of the candidate it is supporting, and it will throw a few logically valid reasons as to why you shouldn't support the other person or party.

A not so good political ad will spend most of its time tearing down the other opponent and lifting up the candidate it's trying to support. While it may use each person's beliefs and policies to do this, they often resort to personal attacks. One example is hearing "He is out to hurt American families but I'm here to help them." Notice how, in addition to being an attack, the ad doesn't mention how the families are being hurt or helped?

At the end of the ad, you should be able to tell who the candidate is, what party they are running for, and what positions they are taking on key issues. Truthfully, a political ad doesn't have to cover the other party at all in order to be effective, but it usually does.

Step 4: Find their Positions

We are told that the candidate is "pro family" but that could mean anything from supporting family-based government programs to drafting anti LGBTQ legislation. A 30-second ad can probably tell you what their stances are, but what specific positions have they taken on bills? What about their opponent?

Look into debates that they've been in, or if they have previous political experience, take a look at their voting history. This will tell you a lot, including if the ad is possibly lying to you. Do the same thing with the opponent. Use the ad as the base of your research. Make it a good place to form questions. Then, let these questions take you further into the research.

Step 5: Locate Logical Fallacies

Finally, watch the ad again. How many logical fallacies can you locate? Common ones include an implicit appeal to ignorance (which you've gotten around thanks to your research), an appeal to hypocrisy, the bandwagon fallacy, circular arguments, and creating a false dilemma. Ad hominem, or personal attacks, are also used in nearly every political ad there is. The more you can find, the more red flags it raises about that candidate. After all, if they have a good platform, why do they need to rely on logical fallacies to trip up their audience?

There are going to be a lot of elections where your choices aren't perfect, but with careful investigation you can make sure that you are actually voting for someone who is going to care about the issues that you do (not just someone who says they do).

Now, politics are easy to cover when it comes to critical thinking, but not everything will be so textbook.

Exercise 2: Analyzing a Health Claim

Here's the thing. Most countries with modern advertising have laws against publishing blatantly untrue information. However, they can twist the facts. Watch this.

Being in the sun for too long can cause cancer. Vitamin D is something that we can partially get from sunlight. Therefore, we can assume that vitamin D can cause cancer.

We know this isn't true, but it could be, and many people know how to twist facts like this.

To make matters worse, many people now create advertisements on social media and the rules are a bit different. Some platforms do have rules against false information, but it's hard to enforce when there are millions of users.

This becomes dangerous when we are dealing with health claims. When we see ads for these, it's important to use a process to ensure that the information you are taking in is real. So, find a health claim and then follow these next steps to decode it!

Step 1: Identify the Claim

First, you should figure out what exactly you are being helped with. The claim should look something like "Problem X can be solved with solution Y." For example, losing weight can be accomplished with the keto diet.

Step 2: Gather the Presented Evidence

What evidence were you given that this worked? Was it testimonials? Trials? Recommendations? Pictures? Third party research? Most health claims will have some research attached to them, but the usefulness of it varies greatly.

Step 3: Evaluate That Evidence

How good is the evidence for the health claim you are analyzing? Generally, we hope that the evidence can strongly back up the claim. Some common forms of evidence have been listed above. Let's see how we might rate them.

First up: testimonials. These are essentially case studies that say that this product has worked for one person. While this is great, there are about eight billion people, and one person (or even a few people) isn't enough to plainly say that something works. It can be a part of the evidence, but there should probably be more to support it.

Next are trials. Now, one trial may have been a fluke, but if the health product has several trials to back up its use, then we know that it works for a significant number of people.

Recommendations are really only great if the person hasn't been paid to recommend it. That data is legally required to be available, and you can usually Google whether or not a person has been paid to recommend a certain product.

Pictures are often used for physical changes, such as on the skin. They can be great, but they are often a part of a testimonial, and they might have been handpicked from a batch. Try to find pictures online rather than what's directly being advertised.

Finally, there is third party research. This is often useful as long as that research holds up to evaluation as well.

Step 4: Consider Alternatives

What other explanations are there for what we are seeing? Go over the data. See if there is anything that might have been unaccounted for.

For example, the keto diet used to be a popular health trend. You would cut out carbs entirely and start to lose weight. At the very beginning, very few considered other explanations. Now, the two that I can think of right away are that the keto diet means eliminating processed foods that often contain chemicals and that it encourages healthier habits, like exercising. Both are just as likely to lead to weight loss.

Step 5: Check For Any Logical Issues

Finally, check things over for bias and logical fallacies.

Exercise 3: Evaluating an Argumentative Essay

For this exercise, you are going to need the essay of one of your friends (we tend to be a little biased if we're using our own work). It can be any essay, as long as it is argumentative. Try not to pick one that they haven't submitted yet. You don't want to be accused of academic dishonesty.

Step 1: Identify the Thesis

Your friend's thesis should identify their main claim and it will likely be in the first paragraph.

Step 2: Gather Their Evidence

In argumentative essays, the evidence should be easy to find, as it's often arranged in paragraph form.

Step 3: Evaluate Their Evidence Against the Claim

Next, check the evidence out. View the sources used for the evidence and see if they are reputable. Your teacher might have required you to use a scientific journal, but even if they haven't, these are usually the best sources if you really want to make sure that the information you're sharing is well supported.

You can also fact-check them to make sure that they all line up. Find some unrelated sources and see if they say the same thing that the first source does. Even if the source is reputable, it's always possible to get something wrong.

Step 4: Consider the Evidence For the Counter Argument

In an argumentative essay, you are often asked to bring up the counter argument and then refute. Was your friend's coverage of the counter argument through, or did they leave anything out? Was it all reputable?

If we purposefully make the counterclaim look weak (a strawman fallacy), people will see right through that. If they are in support of the counterclaim and you haven't touched on the key details that make them believe in it, then they will never be convinced about your side.

Step 5: Evaluate Each Set of Evidence and Compare

Your last step is to score the evidence against each other. Was there enough to sufficiently prove their point? Did they do a good job refuting the counterclaim? These are the questions you are now tasked with answering.

Step 6: Look for Any Bias Or Logical Fallacies

Finally, as with anything involving critical thinking, we have to examine it for bias and logical fallacies. If you find any, try to figure out what they are and be sure to share the information with the writer!

When doing this exercise, you might be able to help your friend on future essays when you share the notes. You can also help yourself. By reviewing these arguments, you are learning how to better write an argumentative essay, and how to argue your point down the line.

Critical thinking can be a lot. It may seem like a lot of work, but it's so important. It gives you a leg up with friends, siblings, authority figures, and especially as you enter the workforce. You will find that the more you do it, the more natural it will become.

Conclusion

The application that critical thinking can have in daily life is insane.

We can use critical thinking for decision making. We are often pressured to make bigger decisions quickly, and regret usually follows. In order to make these decisions well, we need a process for thinking them through. From weighing out the pros and cons of each side of the decision to checking in with yourself after the fact, you are ensuring that you are always thinking it through, making the best decision available to you, and learning from it. When you're trying to decide what to do with your future, critical thinking can help. When you are trying to make a life decision later, this can help with that too. Critical thinking also has the ability to stop people from being able to take advantage of you by getting you to make a big decision on the spot.

Another thing critical thinking can help you with is research and fact-checking. We live in a world where someone has the power to publish something and reach millions of people in a matter of moments. It doesn't have to be true.

We can easily fall for these sites and end up walking around with misinformation that will embarrass us when it does come up. There will be many times where it will become necessary for us to know and understand a topic. We need to be ready for that! Critical thinking helps us go over all of our sources with a fine-tooth comb so that we can make sure we have the best information available to us.

When we are getting information, there is something we need to be careful about. Many issues have two sides and it's not uncommon for people to subtly get you to agree with the side that they believe in most. To do this, they will include bias and logical fallacies in their work and in order to stop the logical errors from swaying our opinion, we need to be able to spot them.

This also matters when we are trying to create our own research and arguments. We need to make sure that it's devoid of bias and logical fallacies and that all of its facts are up to date. If it's not and we are called out on it, we lose credibility.

As you make your way through school, keep trying to hone your critical thinking skills. You can also sharpen them at home through reading, practicing active listening and, in arguments with your parents, understanding their side to either properly refute it or even agree with it.

Some of the most successful people in the world have gotten by thanks to critical thinking skills. Imagine how decision making can come in handy when you are a business executive. Imagine how proper research might make you one of the best marketing agents out there. Imagine being a CEO and sitting in a meeting with a client offering help for your business. What would it mean if you could pick out any logical fallacies? How about finding good research? You might be able to save your company!

Your brain is still developing, so if you start now, you will build the proper structures and that will carry on throughout your adult life. Right now, what would take the average adult a few months might only take you a few weeks to understand. Believe me when I say that you should get started right away.

If this book has been helpful, let everyone know by leaving a review! Let us know if there is anything you would have liked to see included in this book. If you find ways to practice critical thinking that weren't mentioned, then share that too! I wish you luck as you push forward in life!

References

Biases, fallacies, & critical thinking information resources. (n.d.). *Open Education Sociology Dictionary*. Retrieved February 20, 2023, from https://sociologydictionary.org/biases-fallacies-critical-thinking/

Brooks, A. W., & John, L. K. (2018). *The suprising power of questions*. Harvard Business Review. https://hbr.org/2018/05/the-surprising-power-of-questions

Coleman, J. (2022, April 22).*Critical thinking is about asking better questions*. Harvard Business Review. https://hbr.org/2022/04/critical-thinking-is-about-asking-better-questions

Crocket, L. (2021, September 19). *6 benefits of critical thinking and why they matter*. Future Focused Learning. https://blog.futurefocusedlearning.net/critical-thinking-benefits

Fran. (2021, July 9). *How to think critically – a guide to creative and critical thinking*. FutureLearn. https://www.futurelearn.com/info/blog/how-to-think-critically

George, T. (2021, August 26). What are credible sources & how to spot them | examples. Scribbr. https://www.scribbr.com/working-with-sources/credible-sources/

Hanane_Kebbas. (2022, March 2). *Barriers to critical thinking.* Profitiv.com. https://profitiv.com/barriers-to-critical-thinking/

Indeed Editorial Team. (2022, September 30). *10 effective questioning techniques (with tips).* Indeed. https://www.indeed.com/career-advice/career-development/questioning-techniques.

Kubala, J. (2020, June 11). *1,200-calorie diet review: Does it work for weight loss?* Healthline. https://www.healthline.com/nutrition/1200-calorie-diet-review#downsides

Laplante, S. (2022, January 9). *How docial media can crush your self-esteem.*" The Conversation. https://theconversation.com/how-social-media-can-crush-your-self-esteem-174009

Marks, K. (n.d.). *Research basics: How do I know if a source is credible?* Henry Buhl Library. https://hbl.gcc.libguides.com/research/credible

MasterClass. (2021, June 7). *How to identify cognitive bias: 12 examples of cognitive bias.* MasterClass. https://www.masterclass.com/articles/how-to-identify-cognitive-bias

Ocasio-Cortez, A. (n.d.). *About.* Alexandria Ocasio-Cortez. https://ocasio-cortez.house.gov/about

Park, M. (2023, February 22). *Cognitive bias.* Corporate Finance Institute. https://corporatefinanceinstitute.com/resources/capital-markets/list-top-10-types-cognitive-bias/

Ruhl, C. (2023, February 8). *What is cognitive bias? Simple Psychology.* https://simplypsychology.org/cognitive-bias.html

Tawatao, C. (2023, February 27). *Library Guides: FAQ: How do I know if my sources are credible/reliable?* University of Washington Libraries. https://guides.lib.uw.edu/research/faq/reliable

TBS Staff. (2020, June 9). *15 logical fallacies you should know before getting into a debate.* Scribd. www.scribd.com/document/507361356/15-

Jake Johnson

Logical-Fallacies-You-Should-Know-Before-Getting-Into-a-Debate-The-Quad-Magazine

The benefits of critical thinking & how to develop it. (2023, March 1). TSCFM. https://tscfm.org/blogs/the-benefits-of-critical-thinking-for-students/

The Foundation for Critical Thinking. (n.d.). *Defining critical thinking.* The Foundation for Critical Thinking. https://www.criticalthinking.org/template.php?pages_id=766

UMGC. (2022). *The research assignment: How should research sources be evaluated?* University of Maryland Global Campus. https://www.umgc.edu/current-students/learning-resources/writing-center/online-guide-to-writing/tutorial/chapter4/ch4-05

University of the People. (n.d.). *Why is critical thinking important? A survival guide.* University of the People. https://www.uopeople.edu/blog/why-is-critical-thinking-important/

Wiki Contributor. (2023, January 14). *Soundness.* Wikipedia. https://en.wikipedia.org/wiki/Soundness

Willis, J. (2017, January 26). *Donald Trump is making shameless equivocation the dominant form of political discourse.* GQ Daily. https://www.gq.com/story/donald-trump-verbal-tics

Made in the USA
Las Vegas, NV
09 November 2023

80446731R00066